# Machine Learning

---

*Mastering the Basics: An In-Depth Look at Machine Learning*

I always find it wonderful to know when all of Amazon's top books go on free promotion. I'd like to share that with you. Maybe you'll find it wonderful too.

## Click Here For Instant Access

I'd like to say "thank you", and show gratitude. Click above, and you will have full access to an exclusive service that will email you notifications when FREE books from some of Amazon's TOP sellers go on sale. If you are someone who likes quality, especially quality for absolutely free you would love access to this deal.

# Table of Contents

# Introduction

I want to thank you for choosing this book, 'Machine Learning - Mastering The Basics: An In-Depth Look At Machine Learning' and hope you find it informative and interesting in your quest to learn about machine learning.

Since the Industrial Revolution, machines have come a long way. They continue to flood our houses and factories, but it is only in recent times that their capabilities have evolved beyond manual activities. The scope of work for machines has extended to tasks that involve simulating cognition. Until recently, these tasks could only be performed by human beings. Driving cars, judging competitions and beating professional chess players at their game are just a few examples of the complex tasks that machines are now capable of performing.

Some of the remarkable capabilities of machines have started to instill fear among a few observers. Most of the fear nestles on the insecurities that people have about survival, and this fear provokes the following what if questions. What if machines became more intelligent than human beings and decided to fight us? What if they were able to procreate and produce offspring who had capabilities that humans never imparted to machines? What if singularity, which is considered to be a myth, is true?

The other fear that most people have is the threat to job security. If you are a truck driver in the United States, this is a valid fear. According to BBC's interactive online survey, "Will a robot take my job?" job titles like waiters/waitresses, chartered accountants, taxi drivers, bar workers, and receptionists will become automated by the year 2040.

Further research on job automation should always be read with a slight level of skepticism since the future of machines, and artificial intelligence is unknown. Technology is moving fast, but its adoption is an unchartered path with unforeseen challenges. Machine learning is not simple since it does not only involve turning switches on and off. Machine learning is also not an out-of-the-box solution. Machines operate in parallel to the statistical algorithms, which machine learning engineers and data scientists often oversee. Industry experts believe that there could be a time when there will definitely be an inadequate supply of people to operate machines.

Your path to becoming an expert in machine learning probably starts from here. But, you can also satisfy your thirst for knowledge with a base understanding of what machine learning is for now. You do not need to make hasty decisions. Let us proceed with the assumption that you want to train to become a machine learning engineer or data scientist. This book will help you achieve either goal.

The book covers all the information that one would need to gather on machine learning. We will first look at what machine learning entails and also the subjects that it deals with. We will deal with some of these subjects that are linked to machine learning on a broader level at a later stage in the book. The book also talks about different machine learning engineers who work in different fields and how they have used machine learning to enhance their work. I hope their accomplishments will motivate you to want to become an expert in the field of machine learning. Let's begin.

# Chapter 1 - What is Machine Learning?

It is not an easy task to define learning since it includes a wide range of processes. If one were to look into a dictionary for definitions of learning, one would come across phrases such as "to gain knowledge, or understanding of, or skill in, by study, instruction, or experience," and "modification of a behavioral tendency by experience." In a manner similar to the way psychologists study learning in humans, this book will focus on the learning processes of machines. Certainly, the two spheres of animal learning and machine learning are intertwined. A few techniques in machine learning are derived from some techniques used in the former. Also, breakthroughs in machine learning can help in bringing to light a few facets of biological learning.

When it comes to machines, speaking superficially, it can be said that any change to a machine's structure, data stored in memory or composition, to make the machine perform better and have better efficiency, can be the sign of learning in a machine. However, when we go deeper into the field, only a few of these changes can be subsumed into the category of machine learning. For instance, consider a machine that is meant to predict weather forecasts in a certain area for a few weeks. If data about the weather in the area over the past year is added to the memory of the machine, the machine can learn from this data and predict the weather more accurately. This instance can be called machine learning.

To be precise, the field of machine learning applies to machines that are associated with artificial intelligence. Machines associated with artificial intelligence are responsible for tasks such as prediction, diagnosis, recognition, and others. These types of machines "learn" from data that is added to them. This data is called training data because it is used to train the machine. The machines analyze patterns in this data and use these patterns to perform their actions. Machines use different learning mechanisms to analyze the data depending on the actions they are required to perform. These mechanisms can be classified into two broad categories- supervised learning and unsupervised learning.

Skeptics of the field of machine learning might question why machines need to learn in the first place. People may wonder why machines aren't designed specifically for the tasks that they need to carry out. There are many reasons as to why machine learning is advantageous. As mentioned earlier, research into the field of machine learning can help us better understand certain aspects of human learning. Also, machine learning can also increase the accuracy and efficiency of machines. A few other reasons are:

- Even with the greatest efforts by engineers, some tasks cannot be defined explicitly. Some tasks need to be explained to the machine using examples. The idea is to train the machine with the input and teach it how to reach the output. This way, the machine will know how to deal with future inputs and process them to reach appropriate outputs.
- The field of machine learning is also intertwined with the field of data mining. Data mining is essentially the process of looking through loads and loads of data to find important correlations and relationships. This is another advantage of

machine learning in that it might lead to the finding of important information.

- On many occasions, it is possible that humans design machines without correctly estimating the conditions in which it will be functioning. Surrounding conditions can play a huge role on the performance of the machine. In such cases, machine learning can help in the acclimation the machine to its environment so that the performance is not hindered. It is also possible that environmental changes might occur and machine learning will help the machine to adapt to these changes without losing out on performance.
- Another loophole in the process of human beings hardcoding the process into the machine is that the process might be extremely elaborate. In such a case, the programmer might miss out on a few details since it would be a very tedious job to encode all the details. So, it is much more desirable to allow the machine to learn such processes.
- There are constant changes in technology in the world. Major changes occur in other aspects as well such as vocabulary. Redesigning systems to accommodate for each and every change is not practical. Instead, machine-learning methods can be used to train the machines to adapt to these changes.

## Subjects involved in machine learning

The sphere of machine learning is the intersection of many subjects. It derives information from some subjects. Each of these subjects brings in new methodology and terminology. All of these concepts come together to form the discipline of machine learning. Given below are a few of the subjects involved in machine learning.

## Statistics

One of the most common problems in statistics that are used in machine learning is training, i.e., the usage of samples drawn from unknown probability distributions to predict what distribution a new sample is picked from. Another related problem is the estimation of the value of a function at a certain point based on the value of the function at a few sample points. Solutions to these problems are instances of machine learning because the problems involve estimation of future events based on data about past events. Statistics forms an extremely important part of machine learning.

## Brain modelling

The part of brain modeling that is closely related to machine learning is the concept of neural networks. Scientists have suggested that one possible model for neurons or the neural network is non - linear elements with weighted inputs. Extensive studies have been conducted on these non - linear elements in recent times. Scientists concerned with brain modeling are interested in gaining information about human learning from the study of these networks of neurons. Connectionism, sub-symbolic processing, and brain style computation are a few spheres that are associated with these types of studies.

## Adaptive control theory

Control theory is a subject associated with the control of systems. A major problem faced by systems is the change in environmental conditions. Adaptive control theory is a part of this subject that deals with the methods by which systems can adapt to these changes and continue to perform optimally. The main idea is that the systems should anticipate these changes and modify themselves accordingly.

## Psychological modelling

For many years now, psychologists have tried to understand the learning processes of humans. One such example is the EPAM network. This network was used for storing and retrieving one of two words when provided with the other. Later on, the concepts of decision trees and semantic networks were conceived in this field. In recent times, the work in the field of psychology has been strongly influenced by the subject of artificial intelligence. Another aspect of psychology that has been studied in recent times is reinforcement learning. This concept has also been used in machine learning extensively.

## Artificial intelligence

As mentioned earlier, a large part of machine learning is concerned with the subject of artificial intelligence. Studies in artificial intelligence have focused on the usage of analogies for learning purposes and also on how past experiences can help in anticipating and accommodating future events. In recent years, studies have focused on devising rules for systems that use the concepts of inductive logic programming and decision tree methods.

### *Evolutionary models*

It is a common idea in evolutionary studies that not only do animals learn to perform better in life, but they also learn to better adapt to their surroundings to enhance their performance. As far as machines are concerned, the concepts of learning and evolving can be considered to be synonymous with each other. Therefore, models that have been used to explain evolution can be used to devise machine-learning techniques. The most prominent technique that has been developed using evolutionary models is the genetic algorithm.

## Varieties of Machine Learning

So far, this book has given an introduction to machine learning and has answered the question about the subjects that constitute it. Now, we come to the more important question of what can be learned on the subject of machine learning. The following are a few topics on which knowledge can be gained through the study of machine learning:

- Programs and logic rule sets
- Terminology and grammars
- Finite state machines
- Problem - solving systems
- Functions
- Artificial Intelligence
- Statistics

Out of the above, the two most focused on topics are those of statistics and artificial intelligence. These two subjects are used extensively in machine learning. We now move on to chapters that describe the two broad categories of machine learning techniques: supervised machine learning and unsupervised machine learning.

## Uses of Machine Learning

Machine Learning is now a solution to complete manual tasks that are impossible to complete over a short span of time for a large amount of data. In this decade, we are overcome with data and information and have no manual way of processing this information paving the way for automated processes and machines to do that job for us.

Useful information can be derived when the process of analysis and discovery becomes automated. This will help us drive our future actions in an automated process. We have therefore come into the world of Big Data, Business Analytics, and Data Science. Predictive analytics and Business Intelligence are no longer just for the elite but also for small companies and businesses. This has given these small businesses a chance to participate in the process of collecting and utilizing information effectively.

Let us now take a look at some technical uses of machine learning and see how these uses can be applied to real world problems.

### *Density Estimation*

This use of machine learning allows the system to use the data that is provided to create a product that looks similar to it. For instance, if you were to pick up the novel War and Peace from the shelves of a bookstore and run it through a machine, you will be able to make the machine determine the density of the words in the book and provide you with work that is exactly similar to War and Peace.

### Latent Variables

When you work with latent variables, the machine uses the method of clustering to determine whether the variables are related to one another. This is a useful tool when you do not know what the cause of change in different variables is and also when you do not know the relationship between variables. Additionally, when the data set is large, it is better to look for latent variables since that helps to comprehend the data obtained.

### Reduction of Dimensionality

Most often, data obtained has some variables and dimensions. If there are more than three dimensions, it is impossible for the human mind to visualize the data. It is in these instances that machine learning can help in reducing the data into a manageable number of dimensions so that the user understands the relationship between the variables easily.

### Visualization

There are times when the user would just like to visualize the relationship that exists between variables or would like to obtain the summary of the data in a visual form. Machine learning assists in both these processes by summarizing the data for the user using specified or non – specified parameters.

# Chapter 2 - Facts about Machine Learning

Machine learning was once relegated to sci – fi movies about killer robots and machines. Now, machine learning is permeating numerous aspects of our everyday lives, right from optimizing Netflix recommendations to Google searches. Machine learning has contributed to improving different facets of building mechanics in smart building space, and the experiences of the occupant. You do not have to have a Ph.D. to understand the different facets and functions of machine learning. This section covers some facts about machine learning that are very basic and important to know.

## Machine Learning is a subset of Artificial Intelligence

Machine learning is a subset of artificial intelligence that drives the process of data mining. What is the difference between these terms? These terms are often used interchangeably, and experts spend hours debating on where they will need to draw the line between machine learning and artificial intelligence.

Artificial Intelligence can be defined as machines thinking like human beings. The brain can be considered as a computing machine. At any given minute, human beings can capture thousands of data points using the five different senses. The brain can recall memories from the past, draw conclusions based on causes and effects and also make decisions. Human beings learn to recognize patterns, but every being has a limit.

One can think of machine learning as a continuous and automated version of data mining. Data mining is a process that is used to detect certain patterns in data sets that human beings will not be able to find. Machine learning is a process that is capable of reducing the size of the data to detect and extrapolate patterns that will allow us to apply that information to identify new actions and solutions.

In smart building spaces, machine learning enables any building to run efficiently while also responding to occupants' changing needs. For instance, you can consider the difference between how a machine learning application could handle recurring board meetings and how a scheduling program, like a calendar would perform the same task. A scheduling system could be used to adjust the temperatures within the conference room to around 72 degrees on the day of the meeting right before the meeting starts. However, any machine-learning algorithm can make sense of more than a thousand variables at any given time of the year to create an ideal thermal environment during the business meeting.

Both data mining and artificial intelligence have been covered in detail later in the book.

## Machine Learning still requires human assistance

Machine learning helps computers automate, anticipate and evolve but that does not mean that they can take over the world. Machine learning will still need human beings to operate to provide context, to set parameters for operation and also to continue to improve the algorithms being used.

Machine learning helps a computer discover patterns that are not possible for human beings to see. The computer will then make an adjustment to the system. However, it is not good to identify and understand why those patterns exist. For instance, most smart buildings have functions that have been created with the intent to ensure that the people inside the building are more productive. This does not mean that the building can be told that it needs to make people more productive. A human would need to set up the definitions and rules that the building will need to follow.

It is important to note that the data cannot always explain why any anomalies or outliers occur. For instance, an algorithm will always take note and people in a certain area of work continually request the temperature in that area to be reduced by 10 degrees when compared to any other area in the building. The algorithm will not be able to tell the operator this since it will not be able to identify why the temperature is higher in that area of the building. Machine learning did help the operator identify why. Therefore, it is important for skilled people to operate machines to ensure that the conclusions obtained are accurate.

## Two types of Machine Learning

Machine learning can be bifurcated into supervised and unsupervised machine learning. These have been covered in detail in the following chapters. Smart buildings would often incorporate both types. Here is a simple example of how these types of machine learning look like: Let us assume that you want to teach a computer to recognize an ant. When you use a supervised approach, you will tell the computer that an ant is an insect that could either be small or big. You will also need to tell the computer that the ant could either be red or black. When you use an unsupervised approach, you will need to show the computer different animal groups and then tell the computer what an ant looks like and then show the computer another set of pictures and ask it which the ant is till the computer learns the features specific to an ant.

When it comes to smart building spaces, both supervised and unsupervised machine learning are used. Occupant – facing apps are rapidly developed when the cost of sensors used in buildings drops. This helps the occupants provide constructive feedback to the building to continuously correct the building to help it learn to create optimal conditions for the occupants.

## The renaissance of machine learning has begun

During the 1980s there was a rapid development and advancement in computing power and computers. This gave rise to enormous amount of fear and excitement around artificial intelligence, computers and machine learning which could help the world solve a variety of ailments – right from household drudgery to diseases. As artificial intelligence and machine learning developed as formal fields of study, turning these ideas and hopes into reality was more difficult to achieve and artificial intelligence retreated into the world of theory and fantasy. However, in the last decade, the advances in data storage and computing have changed the game again. Tasks that were once considered difficult for machines to learn have now become a reality.

## Most of the work lies in data transformation

When you read through the different techniques of machine learning, you will probably assume that machine learning is mostly about selecting the right algorithm and tuning that algorithm to function accurately. The reality is prosaic – a large chunk of your time goes into cleansing the data and then transforming that data into raw features that would better signal the relationship between your data.

## Deep learning is a revolutionary advance

Deep learning has earned a great name by catering to the advancement of machine learning algorithms and applications. Deep learning works towards automating some of the work through engineering. However, it is not a silver bullet and cannot be used if you have not invested some time in cleansing and transforming the data.

## You do not need a Ph.D. to use machine learning

Writing a machine-learning algorithm is very different from learning how to use that algorithm. After all, you do not need to learn how to program when you use an app on your phone. The best platforms always create an abstract of the program to present the users with an interface that would need minimal training to use. If you do know the basic concepts of machine learning, you are ready to go! It is left to the data scientists to fine tune the algorithms that can be used for a particular case. Users do not need to understand math; they will just need to use the business domain.

Machine learning has come of this age and is growing quickly. Buildings are using machine learning in different ways to make the existing infrastructure efficient and also help to enhance the experience of the occupants residing in the building. Buildings are always learning and analyzing the needs of the occupants, right from energy usage to the environment within the building.

How does this affect us going forward? This advance in machine learning goes to say that most things will happen without the need for us to ask. Machine learning engineering could go beyond managing lighting and temperature. It can be used to adjust calls, screens, shades, signal elevators and shuttles and so on. Machine learning implies that there will be some future state of multiple layers and levels of automation adjusting based on the current activity.

# Chapter 3 - Supervised Machine Learning

As mentioned earlier, an important process of machine learning is called training where the machine is fed with data about past events so that the machine can anticipate future events. When this training data is supervised, it is called supervised machine learning. The data fed essentially consists of training examples. These examples consist of inputs and the desired outputs. These desired outputs are also known as supervisory signals. The machine uses a supervised learning algorithm that generates an inferred function that is used to forecast events. If the outputs are discrete, the function is called a classifier and if the outputs are continuous, the function is known as a regression function. This function is responsible for predicting outputs of future inputs. The algorithm needs to conceive a generalized method of reaching the output from the input based on the previous data. An analogy that can be made in the spheres of human and animal learning is concept learning.

## Overview

Supervised learning is a method that uses a fixed algorithm. Given below are the steps involved in this algorithm:

- The first and foremost step in supervised learning is the determination of the type of examples to be used for training the machine. This is an extremely crucial step and the engineer needs to be very careful in deciding the kind of data he wants to use as examples. For instance, for a speech recognition system, the engineer could either use single words, small sentences or entire paragraphs for training the machine.

- Once the engineer has decided on the type of data he wants to use, he needs to collect data to form a training set. This set needs to be representative of all the possibilities of that function. So, the second step requires the engineer to collect inputs and desired outputs for the training process.

- Now, the next step is to determine how to represent the input data to the machine. This is very important since the accuracy of the machine depends on the input representation of the function. Normally, the representation is done in the form of a vector. This vector contains information about various characteristic features of the input. However, the vector should not include information on too many features since this would increase the time taken for training. A larger number of features might also lead to mistakes made by the machine in prediction. The vector needs to contain exactly enough data to predict outputs.

- After deciding on the representation of input data, a decision must be made on the structure of the function. The learning algorithm to be used must also be decided on. Most commonly used algorithms are decision trees or support vector machines.

- Now the engineer must complete the design. The learning algorithm chosen should be run on the data set that has been gathered for training. Sometimes, certain algorithms require the engineer to decide on some control parameters to ensure that the algorithm works well. These parameters can be estimated by testing on a smaller subset or by using the method of cross validation.

- After running the algorithm and generating the function, the accuracy of the function should be calculated. For this, engineers use a testing set. This set of data is different from the training data and the corresponding outputs to the inputs are already known. The test set inputs are sent to the machine and the outputs obtained are checked with those in the test set.

There are some supervised learning algorithms in use and each one has its strengths and weaknesses. Since there is no definitive algorithm that can be used for all instances, the selection of the learning algorithm is a major step in the procedure.

## Issues to consider in Supervised Learning

With the usage of supervised learning algorithms, there arise a few issues associated with it. Given below are four major issues:

### *Bias-variance tradeoff*

The first issue that needs to be kept in mind while working with machine learning is the bias-variance tradeoff. Consider a situation where we have various but equally good training sets. If when a machine is trained with different data sets, it gives systematically incorrect output predictions for a certain output, the learning algorithm is biased towards that input. A learning algorithm can also be considered to have a high variance for input. This occurs when the algorithm causes the machine to predict different outputs for that input in each training set. The sum of the bias and variance of the learning algorithm is known as the prediction error for the classifier function. There exists a tradeoff between bias and variance. A requirement for learning algorithms with low bias is that they need to be flexible enough in order to accommodate all the data sets. However, if they are too flexible, the learning algorithms might end up giving varying outputs for each training set and hence increases the variance. Supervised learning methods need to be able to adjust this tradeoff. This is generally done automatically or by using an adjustable parameter.

## Function complexity and amount of training data

The second issue is concerned with deciding on the amount of training data based on the complexity of the classifier or regression function to be generated. Suppose the function to be generated is simple, a learning algorithm that is relatively inflexible with low variance and high bias will be able to learn from a small amount of training data. However, on many occasions, the function will be complex. This can be the case due to a large number of input features being involved or due to the machine being expected to behave differently for different parts of the input vector. In such cases, the function can only be learned from a large amount of training data. These cases also require the algorithms used to be flexible with low bias and high variance. Therefore, efficient learning algorithms automatically arrive at a tradeoff for the bias and variance depending on the complexity of the function and the amount of training data required.

## Dimensionality of the input space

Yet another issue that needs to be dealt with is the dimensionality of the input vector space. If the input vector includes a large number of features, the learning problem will become difficult even if the function only considers a few of these features as valuable inputs. This is simply because the extra and unnecessary dimensions could lead to confusion and could cause the learning algorithm to have high variance. So, when the input dimensions are large, the classifier is generally adjusted to offset the effects by having low variance and high bias. In practice, the engineer could manually remove the irrelevant features in order to improve the accuracy and efficiency of the learning algorithm. However, this might not always be a practical solution. In recent times, many algorithms have been developed which are capable of removing unnecessary features and retaining only the relevant ones. This concept is known as dimensionality reduction that helps in mapping input data into lower dimensions in order to improve the performance of the learning algorithm.

## Noise in the output values

The final issue on this list is concerned with the interference of noise in the desired output values. It is possible that the values of the desired outputs (supervisory targets) can be wrong due to the noise that gets added at sensors. These values could also be wrong due to human error. In such cases, the learning algorithm should not look to match the training inputs with their exact outputs. For such cases, algorithms with high bias and low variance are desirable.

## *Other factors to consider*

- One important thing to be kept in mind is the heterogeneity of data. The level of heterogeneity of the data should also play a role in dictating the learning algorithm that is to be chosen. Some algorithms work better on data sets whose inputs are limited within small ranges. A few of these are support vector machines, logistic regression, neural networks, linear regression and nearest neighbor methods. Nearest neighbor methods and support vector machines with Gaussian kernels work especially better with inputs limited to small ranges. On the other hand, there exist algorithms like decision trees that work very well with heterogeneous data sets.
- Another feature of the data sets that need to be considered is the amount of redundancy in the set. A few algorithms perform poorly in the presence of excessive redundancy. This happens due to numerical instabilities. Examples of these types of algorithms are logistic regression, linear regression, and distance based methods. For such cases, regularization needs to be included so that the algorithms can perform better.
- While choosing algorithms, engineers need to consider the amount of non - linearities in the inputs and the interactions within different features of the input vector. If there is little to no interaction and each feature contributes independently to the output, algorithms based on distance functions and linear functions perform very efficiently. However, when there are some interactions within the input features, algorithms based on decision trees and neural

networks are desirable. The reason for this is that these algorithms are designed to detect these interactions in the input vectors. If the engineer decides to use linear algorithms, he must specify the interactions that exist.

When an engineer is tasked with selecting an algorithm for a specific application, he may choose to compare various algorithms experimentally in order to decide which one is best suited for the application. However, a large amount of time needs to be invested by the engineer in collecting training data and tuning the algorithm. If provided with a large number of resources, it is advisable to spend more time collecting data than spending time on tuning the algorithm because the latter is extremely tedious. The most commonly used learning algorithms are neural networks, nearest neighbor algorithms, linear and logistic regressions, support vector machines and decision trees.

# Chapter 4 - Unsupervised Machine Learning

At this point, the reader should be familiar with the concept of supervised machine learning wherein the machine is trained using sets of inputs and outputs that are desired. However, there are other techniques of machine learning. One of these is known as reinforcement learning. In this technique, the machine is designed to interact with its ambient environment through actions. Based on the environment's response to these actions, the machine receives rewards if the environment reacts positively or punishments if it reacts negatively. The machine learns from these reactions and is taught to perform in a manner such that it can maximize the rewards it will obtain in the future. The objective could also be to minimize future punishments. This technique of learning is related to the subjects of control theory in engineering and decision theory in statistics and management sciences.

The main problems studied in these two subjects are more or less equivalent and the solutions are similar as well. However, the two subjects focus on different parts of the problem. There exists another technique of machine learning that is closely related to game theory and also uses reinforcement learning. The idea here is similar to that in reinforcement learning. The machine produces some actions that affect the surrounding environment and it receives rewards or punishments depending on the reaction of the environment. However, the main difference is that the environment is not static. It is dynamic and can include other machines as well. These other machines are also capable of producing actions and receiving rewards (or punishments). So, the objective of the machine is to maximize its future rewards (or minimize its future punishments) taking into account the effects of the other machines in the surroundings.

The application of game theory to such a situation with multiple, dynamic systems is a popular area of research. Finally, the fourth technique is called unsupervised machine learning. In this technique, the machine receives training inputs but it does not receive any target outputs or rewards and punishments for its actions. This begs the question- how can the machine possibly learn anything without receiving any feedback from the environment or having information about target outputs? However, the idea is to develop a structure in the machine to build representations of the input vectors in such a manner that they can be used for other applications such as prediction and decision-making. Essentially, unsupervised learning can be looked at as the machine identifying patterns in input data that would normally go unnoticed. Two of the most popular examples of unsupervised learning are dimensionality reduction and clustering. The technique of unsupervised learning is closely related to the fields of information theory and statistics.

# Chapter 5 - Terms related to Machine Learning

A few terms are often used when it comes to learning machine learning. This chapter covers some of these terms.

## Machine Learning

Although this has been covered in detail above, we will just look at it one more time. Machine learning is concerned with how a computer can be constructed in order to automatically improve the experience of the user. Machine learning is an interdisciplinary science that employs techniques from different fields like computer science, artificial intelligence, mathematics, and statistics and so on. The main aspects of machine learning research include algorithms that help to facilitate this improvement from experience. These algorithms can be applied in some fields like artificial intelligence, data mining and computer vision.

## Fundamental Axioms

Let us take a look at the various axioms that are used in machine learning to understand the math that supports the model. One of the most fundamental axioms can be expressed as follows:

$$0 < P(A) < 1$$

This states that the probability of any event occurring is always going to be greater than zero but less than one, both inclusive. This implies that the probability of the occurrence of any event can never be negative. This makes sense since the probabilities can never be more certain than hundred percent and least certain than zero percent.

## Additive Property

The next axiom that is important to note can only be true when both events A and B are mutually exclusive.

$$P(A+B) = P(A) + P(B)$$

This axiom states that the probability of both events A and B occurring is the same as the sum of the individual probabilities of the events occurring if and only if both events exclude each other. For example, if A is the event that we get a six on rolling a die and B is the event that we get a five rolling a die, then this axiom hold. But, if B were assumed to be the event where we get an even number, this set would include the number six making the axiom false.

## Joint Probability

This property can be expressed as follows:

$$P(a, b) = P(A=a, B=b)$$

This property can be read as the probability of a and b is the same as the probability that event A turns out in state 'a' and event B turns out in state 'b'.

## Bayes' Rule

This rule is often used to identify the conditional probability when P (A, B) is not known. The equation used is as follows:

$$P(A|B) = [P(B|A)*P(A)]/P(B)$$

These various axioms are a great way to understand the logic behind Markov Models. Let us now take a look at the mathematical aspects of the Markov Model. As mentioned above, Markov Models was discovered in the year 1916 by Andreevich Markov, a scientist who was studying and analyzing the frequency of different types of words in Pushkin's poems. These models have now become an integral model to use while working with data science, artificial intelligence, and machine learning.

## Classification

Classification is concerned with separating data into unique classes using models. These models are always built using training data sets for which the classes have already been named in order to help the algorithm learn. Inputting real time data for which the model holds all the classes then uses these models. This will help the model predict the relationship that exists within the data based on what the model has learned from the training dataset. Well – known classification schemes are support vector machines and decision trees. Since these algorithms will need an explicit definition of classes, classification is a form of supervised machine learning.

## Regression

Regression is closely related to classification. Classification is directly concerned with the prediction of discrete classes while regression is applied to datasets where the classes required to be predicted consist of numerical values that are continuous in nature. Linear regression is an example of regression techniques.

## Clustering

Clustering is a technique that is used to analyze data that does not include class attributes or pre-labeled classes within it. The instances in the data are grouped based on the concept of maximizing the similarity within classes and minimize the similarity between classes. This loosely translates into the clustering algorithm that identifies and groups the data instances which are similar to each other while removing any instances, called ungrouped instances that have no similarities to the data. The most well-known clustering algorithm is k – means clustering. Clustering does not require the pre labeling of instance classes; therefore it is a form of unsupervised machine learning meaning that the algorithm learns more from observation as opposed to learning by example.

## Association

Association is easily explained by introducing a market basket analysis, which is a task that it is well – known for. This type of analysis always tries to identify the association that exists between different data instances that have been chosen by any particular shopper and placed in their basket. This could either be real or virtual, and the algorithm always assigns confidence and support measures for comparison. The value of this always lies in customer behavior analysis and cross-marketing. Association algorithms are generalizations of market based analyses and are similar to classification algorithms in the sense that any attribute can be predicted when using association. Apriori is one the best-known association algorithms. If you have deduced that association is an example of unsupervised machine learning, then you are right.

## Decision Trees

Decision trees are recursive, divide and conquer and top-down classifiers. These trees are composed of two main tasks: tree pruning and tree induction. The latter is the task where a set of pre-classified instances are taken as inputs after which decisions are made based on which attributes are split on thereby splitting the dataset and recursing on the resulting split datasets till every training instance has been categorized. While building the tree, the main goal is to split all the attributes to create the child nodes that are pure. This would ensure that the number of splits needed to classify the instances in the dataset, would be few. The purity of the child nodes is always measured based on information gathered which relates to how much information is to be known about a instance that was previously unseen in order to classify it accurately.

A complete decision tree model can always be complex and may contain some unnecessary structure that can be difficult to understand and analyze. Tree pruning helps to remove any unnecessary structure from the decision tree in order to make it easily readable, more efficient and accurate for human beings to comprehend. This increased accuracy due to tree pruning helps to reduce over fitting.

## Deep Learning

Deep learning is a process that has recently gained popularity. This is the process where neural network technology is used to solve different problems. Neural network technology uses neural network architecture where each network has multiple hidden neural networks. These deep neural network architectures are certain machine learning algorithms.

## Support Vector Machines

Support Vector Machines (SVMs) allow the user to classify linear and nonlinear data. They work by transforming the training dataset into higher dimensions that are then inspected for the optimal boundary separation between classes. In SVMs, these boundaries are often referred to as hyper planes which are identified using support vectors or the instances that define the classes and their margins which are the lines that are parallel the hyper planes. These are defined by the shortest distance between the hyper plane and the support vector associated with it.

The goal behind using an SVM is to identify the hyper plane that separates two classes if there are a large number of dimensions. This process helps to delineate the member classes in the dataset. When this process is repeated a number of times, there are enough hyper planes that are generated that can help to separate dimensions in an n − dimension space.

## Generative Model

In statistics and probability, a generative model is used to generate data sets when some parameters are hidden. These models are used in machine learning to either model the data directly or used as an intermediate step to form a conditional probability density function.

# Chapter 6 - Artificial Intelligence and Data Mining

This chapter covers an analysis on what artificial intelligence and data mining entail.

## Artificial Intelligence 101

An amazing development has taken place over the last few years. You may have watched how robots in Star Wars were able to perform so many actions and maybe, just maybe, you would have wondered how wonderful it would have been if this were to happen in this decade. You may not have seen it coming, but this was an inevitable turn of events – the emergence of Artificial Intelligence (AI). Everywhere we look today; we come across some intelligent systems that talk to us – Siri, Google Assistant – offering us advice and also offering us recommendations. These systems improve almost every year to improve its interpretation of images, voice recognitions and also to drive cars based on different techniques used by Facebook and Google's Deep Learning Efforts. Other work always aims to understand and generate machines that would understand our language and communicate with us.

The reemergence of AI has caused a lot of confusion since there are so many companies that have begun to explore the scene. How do we make sense of any of it?

Let us start with a simple definition of AI. Artificial Intelligence or AI is a field of computer science that is aimed at developing computers that are capable of performing tasks that can be done by people, especially those tasks that are considered to be performed by intelligent people.

AI has had some excellent runs. In the early sixties, there were great promises that were made about what a machine could do. In the eighties, it was said to revolutionize the way businesses were run. But in those eras, the promises that were made were too difficult to deliver. So what makes the latest developments in AI any different? What makes the systems developed now any different from the diagnostic programs and neural nets of the past? There are some reasons why the developments in this era are different from the last.

## Increased Computational Resources

The computers we have in this era are faster and can think harder thereby increasing the computational power. The techniques used earlier worked well only in the past, but now there would be a necessity to improve the computational grid and also expand it.

## Deeper Focus

AI has shifted away from looking at smaller aspects of data to look at specific problems. The systems now are capable of thinking about a particular problem as opposed to daydreaming without any problem. Systems like Cortana and Siri work well within limited domains that can be focused and modeled on pulling specific words that you would have said instead of understanding the entire sentence spoken by you.

## Alternative Reasoning Models

Alternative reasoning models have been adopted which are based on the assumption that the systems do not have to reason like human beings in order to be smart. The machine is allowed to think like a machine.

It is these factors put together that have given the world the first renaissance of intelligent machines that have become a part of our lives and have been adopted in different tools and workplaces.

## Knowledge Engineering

The problem and issues with knowledge engineering have been transformed into different aspects of learning. The systems developed these days use their ways to learn. The bottleneck in the systems in the past helped us add more rules to avoid such bottlenecks in the further processing of data. Most approaches in the modern times focus on learning these rules automatically.

## Growth of Data

Over the years, the data collected has increased by a vast amount and this data is being made available to the machines. This increase in the data has given machines much more to think about. This goes to say that learning systems get better at understanding more data and would now be able to look at thousand examples as opposed to only a few hundred.

# Exploring AI

It was mentioned in the final factor above that one of the main differences between developers of AI today and developers of yesteryears is that in today's world, engineers allow most machines to think like machines. The key word here is most. Some developers still look to create machines that are capable of thinking like human beings. The only opposition to this is the doubt about the intentions of the machine. Some people are worried about what machines could be capable of if they could think exactly like human beings.

There are two types of artificial intelligence – strong AI and weak AI.

## *Strong AI*

The sphere of strong AI deals with the development of machines and systems that are capable of thinking like humans. This entails that the machines should be able to reason out and solve problems the way humans do. They should be capable of explaining their solutions as well. Basically, these machines need to have abilities similar to those of human cognition.

## *Weak AI*

As mentioned earlier, people have qualms about designing machines capable of human thinking. So, weak AI deals with the development of machines that work but not at the level of human thinking. Essentially, it deals with the creation of systems and machines that can behave like humans and perform tasks that we can but are devoid of any thinking capabilities that rival human cognition. A great example of such a machine is the Deep Blue made by IBM. The machine became a brilliant chess player but it was unable to explain its moves or show any cognitive abilities.

### *Anything in Between*

In addition to the two types of AI mentioned above, there are certain machines being developed that fall in between the two. These types of systems are capable of learning and can also understand human reasoning. However, they are not subservient to it. The trend in recent times has shifted to these types of machines. The essence of this type of development is to use human cognitive skills and emotions to train the machines but not use them as the models for the machines.

The main conclusion of the previous few paragraphs is that, as opposed to the general consensus from previous times, machines do not have to think like humans to be smart. Machines can think like machines and still be considered Artificial Intelligence.

### *Assessing Data using AI and Machine Learning*

All the major consumer systems around the world are constantly trying to estimate human beings. For instance, online shopping websites such as eBay and Amazon are constantly using machine learning and AI in order to figure out your likes and dislikes so that they can put forth a list of recommendations for you. These machines are trained using the data that you provide them with when you browse and look for products (transactional information). Even webpages like Facebook use this concept in order to recommend pages that you might want to follow.

Using profile data is only a small step in this process. The machines also use information from different categories for training purposes. Recommendation lists can be made better by looking at information such as the area you live in and your budget. These systems also look at the customers who live around you in order to further refine the list of recommendations that are presented to you.

The results of these processes are almost always a group of characteristics:

For instance, if you were someone who just purchased a garden and is looking to grow plants on it, you would probably go online to look for gardening tools. The next time that you would visit that website, you would see recommendations related to gardening. This is how the machine develops that list - it cross-references the products you looked for with products that people have already bought and then looks at what else they purchased. It accesses this list and presents it to you as a recommendations list.

## Data Mining 101

Data mining is a process that is used by numerous businesses to convert the collected raw data into information that can be used by the business. There are specialized tools that can be used to detect patterns in large-scale information which would help you learn more about your consumers and also respond to their concerns while developing strategies that would help to increase your revenue. The ultimate goal of data mining is to increase your profits. Data mining is said to be effective only when data is gathered and stored efficiently and processed in the right manner for future use.

Retail shops, like supermarkets and grocery stores, use data mining the most when compared with larger firms. There are some retailers offering loyalty rewards, which would motivate their customers to purchase only from that retail store since they would be able to reduce their expenditure. These rewards make it easier for the businesses to monitor who is purchasing what product, the time they purchase that product and also their usual budget. After conducting a thorough analysis, the retail store could choose to use the information obtained for different purposes, like providing customer coupons specifically targeted to their purchasing intent and deciding when to place items on sale or when to sell specific products at a higher markup.

### Software

The software that is used for data mining is designed specifically to analyze the relationship within the data and the patterns that emerge from the data according to the needs of the business. For example, data mining software could be used to develop distinct classes of information. Let us take a look at how a grocery store could use data mining. The manager could use the software to understand when it would be the right time to hold a sale for a particular product. The software refers to the data that has been captured and will give the manager a clear idea on the customers' needs and likes. In some instances, data mining specialists may look for clusters of data according to logical relationships, or they study associations and patterns to make conclusions about consumer trends.

## Strategies

There are different kinds of analysis that can be performed by businesses in order to obtain valuable data. There are different types of business data analytics that could be used to obtain different results each of which will impact the business differently. The type of strategy that needs to be used depends fully on the business and the kind of problem that the business is trying to address.

There are different forms of data analytics that could result in different outcomes thereby offering different insights on the data obtained by the business. One of the best ways to retrieve insights from data is through the process of data mining.

When it comes to developing the data analytics strategy, it is important to understand the definition of data mining and also understand how crucial it is to your business. It is important to take note that the goal of any data mining process is to look for relevant information that would be easily understood when looking at large scale data sets.

Below are the most common types of data mining analytics that you can use for your business.

### Anomaly Detection

Anomaly detection is the process of searching for information in a data set that does not match the expected behavior of the pattern that was predicted. Anomalies are also known as contaminants, exceptions, surprises and most commonly, outliers. They often offer information that is crucial. Outliers are certain parts of the data set that deviate considerably from the general average of the data set thereby causing a hindrance to the analysis. When looked at in numerical terms, these outliers are separate from the rest of the data and could signify that further analysis would need to be made to better understand the data.

Detecting anomalies in data sets could be used to identify if there are risks or frauds that are taking place within crucial systems. These outliers or anomalies have properties that would attract the attention of a data analyst who would then delve deeper to understand what is happening within the data set. This will help the business identify some crucial situations that indicate fraud, flaws in processes and also flaws in strategies used by the business.

It is important to take note that in large data sets, there are definitely going to be some anomalies. It is true that anomalies show bad data, but it is also true that these anomalies could be caused due to random variation and may not affect the data badly. In such situations, it is necessary to conduct more analysis.

### Association Analysis

Association analysis helps the business identify the associations that exist between different variables in a large-scale data set. This strategy will allow the data analyst discover patterns that are concealed within the data which would help to identify variables inside the data and also understand the occurrences of some variables within the data set.

This strategy is commonly used in retail stores to identify patterns that are found within the data set or information from POS. These patterns can come in handy when it comes to identifying or recommending new products to other managers of the same retail store or to loyal customers based on what has been purchased before at the store. If you do this correctly, you will be able to increase your business's conversion rate and also increase your profits.

A good example would be that of Walmart's use of data mining since 2004. The retail giant discovered that the sale of Strawberry pops had increased by at least seven times before the hurricane. In response to this finding, the retail store placed this product at checkout counters when the hurricane was to strike in a particular area.

### *Regression Analysis*
Regression analysis is used to determine the dependency, if any, between the different attributes in a data set. There is an assumption that one variable could elicit a response from another variable thereby causing a change in the data set.

Attributes that are often assumed to be independent could be affected by each other that would mean that a dependency is created between them. By using regression analysis, the business owner will be able to identify if one variable is dependent on another variable and if there is any mutual dependency between the two.

A business can use regression analysis to identify and determine the levels of satisfaction of a client and how well this attribute can impact customer loyalty and also how the service could be affected.

Another good example to look at is the information collected by dating sites. They use regression analysis to offer better services to their users. For instance, if you have a Tinder account, the data provided by you is matched against the data provided by another member on tinder. If there is any dependency between these variables, you will find that person's profile on your feed.

Data mining could help businesses look for and focus on the most relevant and important information, which could be used to establish models that could help in making projections on how systems or people could behave so the business could make some projections.

When more data is gathered, better models can be built which would help you use the strategies in better ways resulting in a greater value for your business.

### Clustering Analysis

The process of detecting data sets within data sets that have similar attributes is called clustering analysis. This type of analysis helps you identify the similarities and the differences between the data collected. Every cluster has a specific trait that would be used to enhance any algorithms that have been created by the business. For example, there could be customers who would often purchase the same products from the store and these customers could be grouped into a cluster. This cluster could be targeted and analyzed by the data analysts to increase the revenue for a firm.

An outcome of clustering analysis is the development of customer personas that can then be used to represent different customer types within a particular data set. This includes the behavior set or attitude of customers who are using the brands or products. The business can use a particular software or programming language to work on relevant cluster analysis.

## Data Science 101

Data science is an emerging area or field in statistics that are associated with the collection, preparation, analysis, visualization, management, and development of vast amounts of data or information. The term Data Science does refer and connect strongly with such areas as computer science and databases, but some other skills are required, including non-mathematical skills.

For some, the term "data science" conjures an image of a statistician in a white lab coat, staring at the computer screen and scrolling through numbers. This is anything but the truth. First, statisticians do not wear coats – this is a statement of fashion that is reserved for biologists, doctors, and scientists who will need to keep their clothes clean when in environments filled with fluids. Second, most of the data that is collected is unstructured and non-numeric, implying that the data is not found in rows and columns and could be in any form – text, video, or audio. Think about a website that is filled with pictures and messages from friends or other users – there is absolutely no way you can find numbers on that page.

It is true that most companies, governments, and schools use plenty of information in the form of numbers – sales, grades, tax assessments – but there is a lot of information in this world that makes mathematicians and statisticians cringe! It is useful to have someone who has kick-ass mathematics skills, but there is more to data than just math. It is important that people working on data are comfortable with words, paragraphs, lists, images, sounds, videos, and any other forms of information.

In addition to this, data science is more than just the analysis and management of the data or information obtained. There are a large number of people who enjoy analyzing data and would love to spend hours looking at histograms and plots, but for those who prefer more than just that, there are some roles offered by data science that cater to different skills. Let us take a look at the different types of data that would be involved when it comes to buying a particular kind of cereal.

No matter what your preferences are for cereal – chocolaty, fruity, fibrous, or nutty – you just prepare to purchase a box of cereal by writing cereal on your shopping list. This plan purchase is a piece of data even though it is just a small scribble on a sheet of paper. When you reach the grocery store, this list is what helps you buy a box of cereal and put it in your cart. At the checkout, the cashier will scan the barcode of the product, and the cash register would log the price. In the data warehouse, the computer will tell the stock manager that the stock for that particular box of cereal has reduced by one. You have a coupon for your box, and the cashier will scan this and give you a discount on the box. At the end of the day or week, the information concerning the cereal would get uploaded to the cereal company, which would then reimburse the grocery store for all the coupons handed out to their customers. Finally, at the end of the month, the store manager would create colorful pie charts and graphs that show the different kinds of cereal that were sold at the warehouse. This would help the manager decide what types of cereal they should stock their shelves with.

The small piece of data that started out with a small sheet of paper has now ended up in different places. It may have ended up on the manager's desk, based on which he or she will need to decide on whether or not to use that brand of cereal. The data went on a long trip from the tip of your pencil to the manager's desk. However, this data would not have been sent to the manager's desk without any transformation. In addition to the different computers used and the software on those computers, other hardware, such as the barcode scanner, comes into the picture. All of these put together will help to scan, collect, manipulate, transmit, and store the data, which would then be analyzed by the manager.

It is obvious that data scientists are not a part of each step in the process. They do not build the hardware that is used to collect the information. So where do they come into the picture? Data scientists would play the most active role in the following aspects: Data Architecture, Data Acquisition, Data Analysis, and Data Archiving, also called the four A's of data. Let us continue to look at the cereal example. With respect to architecture, it is important in the design of the "sale" system to think in advance how people would make use of the data that is coming out of the system. The system architect would have a keen appreciation that both the stock and store manager would need to use the data that is scanned at the cash register for similar purposes. A data scientist would help the architect by providing input on how the data would be used and how it would need to be routed and organized to support the visualization, analysis, and presentation of the data to the right people.

Next, acquisition focuses on how the data is to be collected and how it would need to be represented in the analysis of the data when it begins. For instance, every bar code accounts for a number that does not describe the product itself. At what point must the barcode be associated with the description of the product that it was printed on? Different bar codes are used for the same product. When should we make a note of the fact that both Products X and Y are the same but have different bar codes? Representation, transforming, grouping, and linking of data are all tasks that will need to be performed before so that the data can be analyzed for profitability. These are the tasks in which the data scientist is involved.

The analysis phase is where the data scientist is most involved. In this context, we would be using analysis to summarize the data that was collected, using certain segments of the data to make inferences about the data as a whole. This report would then be presented in tables, graphs, charts, and animations. There are many technical, statistical, and mathematical aspects of these activities, but it is important to remember that the ultimate audience for data analysis is, in fact, a person or a group of individuals. These people are the data users, and it is these people's needs that data scientists would be fulfilling. This point highlights the need for excellent communication skills in data science. The most sophisticated statistical analysis developed would not be worth anything unless the results that have been created can be communicated effectively to the data user.

Finally, data scientists will need to become involved in the archiving of the data. The preservation of collected information in a form that will make it useful in the future – you can term this as data curation – is a difficult challenge because it's hard to anticipate the future uses of data. For instance, when the developers of Twitter were working on how to store tweets, they never expected that these tweets could be used to pinpoint earthquakes and tsunamis, but they had enough foresight to realize that these "geocodes" could be useful elements to store as data.

# Chapter 7 - Noted Experts

Machine learning is an incredibly varied and broad field with a variety of applications. Some of these applications have been covered in the previous chapter. Therefore, writing a list entitled "Noted Experts" is extremely challenging for numerous reasons.

Firstly, the experts mentioned in this chapter are those who are currently working in the field. It has not been extended to include those who have passed since the list would never end.

Secondly, this list cannot be ranked, since one cannot decide which of these experts is more remarkable. How would you decide which expert has made a better discover?

Third, this list is not an exhaustive list of the people currently making significant discoveries and contributions to the field of machine learning or the world. You may find other experts who have made other discoveries if you read through the information on the Internet.

## Geoffrey Hinton

It is very hard, to sum up the discoveries and research studies that have been conducted by these extraordinary minds in a couple of sentences, and this proves to be incredibly hard with Hinton. Hinton had already been making his mark on deep learning three decades ago. He co–invented the back propagation, Boltzmann machines and contrastive divergence. However, it was only when computing power had managed to meet the demands of deep learning that Hinton began to gain the wider recognition that he deserved.

In 2004, he co − founded a group of researchers from across different fields of physics, engineering and neuroscience called Neural Computation and Adaptive Perception. He also founded a company called DNNResearch, which was acquired by Google a year ago. He has been working on the "Brain" project with Google using neural networks since then and has been trying to improve image recognition for Google and also improve audio recognition capabilities of Android.

## Michael I Jordan

Michael, I Jordan is currently working as a professor at UC Berkeley. His research interests and teaching are split between EECS and Statistics. He worked towards the increased use of Bayesian networks in the algorithms and applications developed for machine learning and also played a pivotal role in bringing the overlap between statistics and machine learning to the attention of a larger audience. His graduate and post doctorate students, some of whom are on the list, have gone on to influence the machine learning industry profoundly.

## Andrew Ng

Andrew Ng is Michael I Jordan's student. He currently works as an Associate Professor at Stanford and is also the Director of Stanford's Intelligence Lab. He was the former chief scientist at Baidu. He co-authored and authored some papers on artificial intelligence and machine learning. He was the brains behind the Autonomous Helicopter project at Stanford. The helicopter was developed through reinforcement learning, which is an area of machine learning that is inspired by behavioral psychology.

## Daphne Koller

Daphne Koller is a professor of Computer Science at Sanford University. She completed her masters from the Hebrew University of Jerusalem at the age of 18 and had since gone on to become a recipient of the McArthur Fellowship. Her work focuses on inference, learning, representation, decision making and has recently taken onto studying computer vision and computational biology. She also co-founded Coursera.

Click here to share your thoughts. Pros or cons help improve the quality of this book.

# Conclusion

Machine learning has earned a great deal of importance over the last few years. People from different fields have begun to research how they can incorporate machine learning in their field of study. Therefore, it is of utmost importance to understand what machine learning is and how it is linked to different fields of study.

This book provides you with all the information you would need on machine learning. You will gather an idea on the different subjects that are linked to machine learning and some facts about machine learning that make it an interesting subject to learn. Machine learning has been linked to artificial intelligence and data mining since the beginning of time. Hence, it is important to gather some information about these fields of study too. The book gives you an overview of the fields and also talks about an extension of machine learning, which is data science.

Thank you for purchasing the book. I hope you have gathered all the information necessary for machine learning.

I always find it wonderful to know when all of Amazon's top books go on free promotion. I'd like to share that with you. Maybe you'll find it wonderful too.

## Click Here For Instant Access

I'd like to say "thank you", and show gratitude. Click above, and you will have full access to an exclusive service that will email you notifications when FREE books from some of Amazon's TOP sellers go on sale. If you are someone who likes quality, especially quality for absolutely free you would love access to this deal.

I'd like to ask ONE favor of you. This is more so for future readers of this book. Please take the time to leave an HONEST review of this book. Share what you enjoyed. Share what could be improved. This book like all my books will continually be updated to make sure the upmost quality is circulating.

http://bit.ly/Machinelea

www.ingramcontent.com/pod-product-compliance
Lightning Source LLC
Chambersburg PA
CBHW061037050326
40689CB00012B/2875